I0753375

30 CTS.] [No. 3.

THE

COTTAGE LIBRARY.

"UNDER GREEN LEAVES."

A BOOK OF RURAL POEMS.

EDITED BY

RICHARD HENRY STODDARD.

Illustrated.

NEW-YORK: BUNCE & HUNTINGTON

THE COTTAGE LIBRARY.

"INFINITE RICHES IN LITTLE ROOM."

THE Subscribers have commenced the issue of a Series of attractive hand-volumes, containing choice Selections from Standard Authors, issued at a low price, but in elegant style, and designed for popular circulation. Each volume will be handsomely illustrated, and printed on fine paper. 96 pages, 16mo, paper covers, with Vignette Title. Price 30 cts. each. Now ready:—

I.

HOME BALLADS BY OUR HOME POETS.

WITH ILLUSTRATIONS BY F. O. C. DARLEY.

II.

THE SONG OF THE SHIRT, AND OTHER POEMS.

BY THOMAS HOOD. WITH ILLUSTRATIONS.

In Press,

"UNDER GREEN LEAVES:" A BOOK OF RURAL POEMS.
ILLUSTRATED.

FAVORITE POEMS, BY ENGLISH AUTHORS.

FAMOUS LOVE POEMS.

BUNYAN'S PILGRIM'S PROGRESS.

VICAR OF WAKEFIELD,
ETC., ETC.

BUNCE & HUNTINGTON, PUBLISHERS,
NO. 540, BROADWAY, NEW YORK.

"UNDER GREEN LEAVES."

A BOOK OF RURAL POEMS.

EDITED BY

RICHARD HENRY STODDARD.

"Annihilating all that's made
To a green thought in a green shade."

ANDREW MARVELL.

NEW YORK:
BUNCE & HUNTINGTON.
1865.

CONTENTS.

"UNDER GREEN LEAVES."

SONG.

UNDER the greenwood tree
Who loves to lie with me,
And tune his merry note
Unto the sweet bird's throat,
Come hither, come hither, come hither;
Here shall he see
No enemy
But Winter and rough weather.

Who doth ambition shun,
And loves to live i' the sun,
Seeking the food he eats,
And pleased with what he gets,
Come hither, come hither, come hither;
Here shall he see
No enemy
But Winter and rough weather.

William Shakspeare.

THE GREENWOOD.

OH! when 'tis summer weather,
And the yellow bee, with fairy sound,
The waters clear is humming round,
And the cuckoo sings unseen,
And the leaves are waving green—
Oh! then 'tis sweet,
In some retreat,
To hear the murmuring dove,
With those whom on earth alone we love,
And to wind through the greenwood together.

But when 'tis winter weather,
And crosses grieve,
And friends deceive,
And rain and sleet
The lattice beat—
Oh! then 'tis sweet
To sit and sing
Of the friends with whom, in the days of Spring,
We roamed through the greenwood together.

W. L. Bowles.

SUMMER WOODS.

COME ye into the summer woods;
There entereth no annoy;
All greenly wave the chestnut leaves,
And the earth is full of joy.

I cannot tell you half the sights
  Of beauty you may see,
The bursts of golden sunshine,
  And many a shady tree.

There, lightly swung, in bowery glades,
  The honey-suckles twine;
There blooms the rose-red campion,
  And the dark-blue columbine.

There grows the four-leaved plant, "true love,"
  In some dusk woodland spot;
There grows the enchanter's night-shade,
  And the wood forget-me-not.

And many a merry bird is there,
  Unscared by lawless men;
The blue-winged jay, the woodpecker,
  And the golden-crested wren.

Come down, and ye shall see them all,
  The timid and the bold;
For their sweet life of pleasantness,
  It is not to be told.

And far within that summer wood,
  Among the leaves so green,
There flows a little gurgling brook,
  The brightest e'er was seen.

There come the little gentle birds,
  Without a fear of ill,
Down to the murmuring water's edge,
  And freely drink their fill!

And dash about and splash about,
  The merry little things;
And look askance with bright black eyes,
  And flirt their dripping wings.

I've seen the freakish squirrels drop
  Down from their leafy tree,
The little squirrels with the old,—
  Great joy it was to me!

And down unto the running brook,
  I've seen them nimbly go;
And the bright water seemed to speak
  A welcome kind and low.

The nodding plants they bowed their heads,
  As if in heartsome cheer:
They spake unto these little things,
  "'Tis merry living here!"

Oh, how my heart ran o'er with joy!
  I saw that all was good,
And how we might glean up delight
  All round us, if we would!

And many a wood-mouse dwelleth there,
  Beneath the old wood shade,
And all day long has work to do,
  Nor is of aught afraid.

The green shoots grow above their heads,
  And roots so fresh and fine
Beneath their feet; nor is there strife
  'Mong them for mine and thine.

There is enough for every one,
  And they lovingly agree;
We might learn a lesson, all of us,
  Beneath the greenwood tree.

Mary Howitt.

IN THE WOOD.

In the wood, where shadows are deepest
  From the branches overhead,
Where the wild wood-strawberries cluster,
  And the softest moss is spread,
I met to-day with a fairy,
  And I followed her where she led.

Some magical words she uttered
  I alone could understand,
For the sky grew bluer and brighter,
  While there rose on either hand
The cloudy walls of a palace
  That was built in Fairy-land.

And I stood in a strange enchantment;
  I had known it all before:
In my heart of hearts was the magic
  Of days that will come no more—
The magic of joy departed,
  That Time can never restore.

That never, ah, never, never,
  Never again can be.
Shall I tell you what powerful fairy

Built up this palace for me?
It was only a little white Violet
I found at the root of a tree.

Adelaide Anne Proctor.

When in the woods I wander all alone,
The woods, that are my solace and delight,
Which I more covet than a Prince's throne,
My toil by day, my canopy by night
(Light heart, light foot, light food, and slumber light,
These lights shall light us to old Age's gate,
While monarchs, whom rebellious dreams affright,
Heavy with fear, death's fearful summons wait);
Whilst here I wander, pleased to be alone,
Weighing in thought the World's no happiness,
I cannot choose but wonder at its moan,
Since so plain joys the woody life can bless.
Then live who may, where honeyed words prevail;
I with the deer, and with the nightingale!

Lord Thurlow.

UNDER THE TREES.

When the summer days are bright and long,
And the little birds pipe a merry song,
'Tis sweet in the shady woods to lie,
And gaze at the leaves, and the twinkling sky,

Drinking the while the rare, cool breeze,
Under the trees—under the trees!

When winter comes, and the days are dim,
And the wind is singing a mournful hymn,
'Tis sweet in the faded woods to stray,
And tread the dead leaves into the clay,
Thinking of all life's mysteries,
Under the trees—under the trees!

Summer or winter, day or night,
The woods are an ever-new delight;
They give us peace, and they make us strong,
Such wonderful balms to them belong;
So, living or dying, I'll take mine ease
Under the trees—under the trees!

Anonymous.

SONG IN PRAISE OF SPRING.

When the wind blows
    In the sweet rose-tree,
And the cow lows
    On the fragrant lea,
And the stream flows
    All light and free,
    'Tis not for me, 'tis not for thee;
'Tis not for any *one* here, I trow:
    The gentle wind bloweth,
    The happy cow loweth,
    The merry stream floweth,
For all below!

O the Spring! the bountiful Spring!
She shineth and smileth on every thing.

Where come the sheep?
To the rich man's moor.
Where cometh sleep?
To the bed that's poor.
Peasants must weep,
And kings endure;
This is a fate that none can cure:
Yet Spring doeth all she can, I trow;
She bringeth the bright hours,
She weaveth the sweet flowers,
She dresseth her bowers,
For all below!
O the Spring! the bountiful Spring!
She shineth and smileth on every thing.

Barry Cornwall.

SONG.

Now the lusty Spring is seen
Golden yellow, gaudy blue.
Daintily invite the view.
Everywhere, on every green,
Roses blushing as they blow
And enticing men to pull,
Lilies whiter than the snow,
Woodbines, of sweet honey full:
All love's emblems, and all cry,
"Ladies, if not plucked, we die."

Yet the lusty Spring hath stayed;
  Blushing red and purest white
  Daintily to love invite
Every woman, every maid.
Cherries kissing as they grow,
  And inviting men to taste,
Apples even ripe below,
  Winding gently to the waist:
    All love's emblems, and all cry,
    "Ladies, if not plucked, we die."

Beaumont and Fletcher.

LINES WRITTEN IN EARLY SPRING.

I HEARD a thousand blended notes,
  While in a grove I sat reclined,
In that sweet mood when pleasant thoughts
  Bring sad thoughts to the mind.

To her fair works did Nature link
  The human soul that through me ran;
And much it grieved my heart to think
  What man has made of man.

Through primrose tufts, in that green bower,
  The periwinkle trailed its wreaths;
And 'tis my faith that every flower
  Enjoys the air it breathes.

The birds around me hopped and played,
  Their thoughts I cannot measure:
But the least motion which they made,
  It seemed a thrill of pleasure.

The budding twigs spread out their fan
  To catch the breezy air;
And I must think, do all I can,
  That there was pleasure there.

If this belief from heaven be sent,
  If such be Nature's holy plan,
Have I not reason to lament
  What man has made of man?

William Wordsworth.

SONG OF SPRING.

Laud the first spring daisies;
Chant aloud their praises;
Send the children up
To the high hill's top;
Tax not the strength of their young hands
To increase your lands.
Gather the primroses,
Make handfuls into posies;
Take them to the little girls who are at work in mills:
Pluck the violets blue—
Ah, pluck not a few!
Knowest thou what good thoughts from Heaven the violet instils?

Give the children holidays
(And let these be jolly days),
Grant freedom to the children in this joyous spring;
Better men, hereafter,
Shall we have, for laughter

Freely shouted to the woods, till all the echoes ring.
Send the children up
To the high hill's top,
Or deep into the wood's recesses,
To woo Spring's caresses.

See the birds together,
In this splendid weather,
Worship God—(for he is God of birds as well as men):
And each feathered neighbor
Enters on his labor—
Sparrow, robin, redpole, finch, the linnet, and the wren;
As the year advances,
Trees their naked branches
Clothe, and seek your pleasure in their green apparel.
Insect and wild beast
Keep no Lent, but feast;
Spring breathes upon the earth, and their joy's increased,
And the rejoicing birds break forth in one loud carol.

Ah, come and woo the Spring;
List to the birds that sing;
Pluck the primroses; pluck the violets;
Pluck the daisies,
Sing their praises;
Friendship with the flowers some noble thought begets.
Come forth and gather these sweet elves
(More witching are they than the fays of old),
Come forth and gather them yourselves;
Learn of these gentle flowers, whose worth is more, than gold.

Come, come into the wood;
Pierce into the bowers
Of these gentle flowers,
Which not in solitude
Dwell, but with each other keep society:
And with a simple piety,
Are ready to be woven into garlands for the good.
Or, upon summer earth,
To die, in virgin worth;
Or to be strewn before the bride,
And the bridegroom, by her side.

Come forth on Sundays;
Come forth on Mondays;
Come forth on any day;
Children, come forth to play:—
Worship the God of Nature in your childhood;
Worship Him at your tasks with best endeavor;
Worship Him in your sports; worship Him ever;
Worship Him in the wildwood;
Worship Him amidst the flowers;
In the greenwood bowers;
Pluck the buttercups, and raise
Your voices in His praise!

Edward Youl.

SONG.

When daisies pied, and violets blue,
And lady-smocks all silver white,
And cuckoo-buds of yellow hue,

Do paint the meadows with delight,
The cuckoo then, on every tree,
Mocks married men, for thus sings he:
Cuckoo;
Cuckoo, cuckoo,—O word of fear,
Unpleasing to a married ear!

When shepherds pipe on oaten straws,
And merry larks are ploughmen's clocks,
When turtles tread, and rooks and daws,
And maidens bleach their summer smocks,
The cuckoo then, on every tree,
Mocks married men, for thus sings he:
Cuckoo;
Cuckoo, cuckoo,—O word of fear,
Unpleasing to a married ear!

William Shakspeare.

TO DAFFODILS.

Fair daffodils! we weep to see
You haste away so soon;
As yet the early-rising sun
Has not attained his noon:
Stay, stay
Until the hastening day
Has run
But to the even-song;
And, having prayed together, we
Will go with you along.

We have short time to stay as you;
We have as short a Spring;

As quick a growth to meet decay,
As you, or any thing:
We die,
As your hours do; and dry
Away
Like to the summer's rain,
Or as the pearls of morning dew,
Ne'er to be found again.

Robert Herrick.

TO BLOSSOMS.

Fair pledges of a fruitful tree,
Why do ye fall so fast?
Your date is not so past
But you may stay yet here awhile
To blush and gently smile,
And go at last.

What! were ye born to be
An hour or half's delight,
And so to bid good-night?
'Tis pity Nature brought ye forth
Merely to show your worth,
And lose you quite.

But you are lovely leaves, where we
May read how soon things have
Their end, though ne'er so brave;
And, after they have shown their pride,
Like you, awhile, they glide
Into the grave.

Robert Herrick.

TO PRIMROSES,

FILLED WITH MORNING DEW.

Why do ye weep, sweet babes? Can tears
Speak grief in you,
Who were but born
Just as the modest morn
Teemed her refreshing dew?
Alas! ye have not known that shower
That mars a flower;
Nor felt th' unkind
Breath of a blasting wind;
Nor are ye worn with years;
Or warped, as we,
Who think it strange to see
Such pretty flowers, like to orphans young,
Speaking by tears before ye have a tongue.

Speak, whimpering younglings, and make known
The reason why
Ye droop and weep.
Is it for want of sleep,
Or childish lullaby?
Or, that ye have not seen as yet
The violet?
Or brought a kiss
From that sweetheart to this?
No, no; this sorrow, shown
By your tears shed,
Would have this lecture read:—
"That things of greatest, so of meanest worth,
Conceived with grief are, and with tears brought forth.'

Robert Herrick.

THE PRIMROSE.

Welcome, pale primrose! starting up between
  Dead matted leaves of ash and oak, that strew
  The every lawn, the wood, and spinny through,
Mid creeping moss and ivy's darker green;
  How much thy presence beautifies the ground!
How sweet thy modest, unaffected pride
Glows on the sunny bank, and wood's warm side!
  And where thy fairy flowers in groups are found,
The school-boy roams enchantedly along,
  Plucking the fairest with a rude delight;
While the meek shepherd stops his simple song
  To gaze a moment on the pleasing sight;
O'erjoyed to see the flowers that truly bring
The welcome news of sweet returning Spring.

John Clare.

SONG: ON MAY MORNING.

Now the bright morning star, day's harbinger,
Comes dancing from the east, and leads with her
The flowery May, who from her green lap throws
The yellow cowslip, and the pale primrose.
  Hail, bounteous May, that dost inspire
  Mirth, and youth, and warm desire!
  Woods and groves are of thy dressing,
  Hill and dale doth boast thy blessing.
  Thus we salute thee with our early song,
  And welcome thee, and wish thee long.

John Milton.

SONG TO MAY.

May! queen of blossoms,
  And fulfilling flowers,
With what pretty music
  Shall we charm the hours?
Wilt thou have pipe and reed,
Blown in the open mead?
Or to the lute give heed
  In the green bowers?

Thou hast no need of us,
  Or pipe or wire,
That hast the golden bee
  Ripened with fire;
And many thousand more
Songsters, that thee adore,
Filling earth's grassy floor
  With new desire.

Thou hast thy mighty herds,
  Tame, and free livers;
Doubt not, thy music too
  In the deep rivers;
And the whole plumy flight,
Warbling the day and night—
Up at the gates of light,
  See, the lark quivers!

When with the jacinth
  Coy fountains are tressed;

And for the mournful bird
  Greenwoods are dressed,
That did for Tereus pine;
Then shall our songs be thine,
To whom our hearts incline:
  May, be thou blessed!

Lord Thurlow.

THE QUEEN OF THE MAY.

HERE'S a bank with rich cowslips and cuckoo-buds strewn,
  To exalt your bright looks, gentle Queen of the May!
Here's a cushion of moss for your delicate shoon,
  And a woodbine to weave you a canopy gay.

Here's a garland of red maiden-roses for you—
  Such a delicate wreath is for beauty alone;
Here's a golden king-cup, brimming over with dew,
  To be kissed by a lip just as sweet as its own.

Here are bracelets of pearl from the fount in the dale,
  That the nymph of the wave on your wrists doth bestow;
Here's a lily-wrought scarf your sweet blushes to hide,
  Or to lie on that bosom, like snow upon snow.

Here's a myrtle enwreathed with a jessamine band,
  To express the fond twining of beauty and youth;
Take this emblem of love in thy exquisite hand,
  And do thou sway the evergreen sceptre of Truth.

Then around you we'll dance, and around you we'll
sing—
To soft pipe and sweet tabor we'll foot it away;
And the hills, and the dales, and the forests shall ring,
While we hail you our lovely young Queen of the May.

George Darley.

SONG.

Pack clouds away, and welcome day,
With night we banish sorrow:
Sweet air, blow soft; mount, lark, aloft,
To give my love good-morrow.
Wings from the wind to please her mind,
Notes from the lark I'll borrow:
Bird, prune thy wing; nightingale, sing,
To give my love good-morrow.
To give my love good-morrow,
Notes from them all I'll borrow.

Wake from thy nest, robin redbreast,
Sing, birds, in every furrow;
And from each hill let music shrill
Give my fair love good-morrow.
Blackbird and thrush in every bush,
Stare, linnet, and cock-sparrow,
You pretty elves, amongst yourselves,
Sing my fair love good-morrow.
To give my love good-morrow,
Sing, birds, in every furrow.

Thomas Heywood.

TO A SKYLARK.

Up with me, up with me, into the clouds!
  For thy song, lark, is strong,
Up with me, up with me, into the clouds!
      Singing, singing,
With clouds and sky about thee ringing,
  Lift me, guide me, till I find
  The spot which seems so to thy mind!

I have walked through wildernesses dreary,
And to-day my heart is weary;
Had I now the wings of a Faery,
  Up to thee would I fly.
There is madness about thee, and joy divine
In that song of thine;
  Lift me, guide me, high and high,
  To thy banqueting-place in the sky.

Joyous as morning,
Thou art laughing and scorning:
Thou hast a nest for thy love and thy rest,
  And, though little troubled with sloth,
  Drunken lark! thou wouldst be loath
To be such a traveller as I.
Happy, happy Liver,
With a soul as strong as a mountain river,
Pouring out praise to the Almighty Giver,
  Joy and jollity be with us both!

Alas! my journey, rugged and uneven,
  Through prickly moors or dusty ways must wind;
  But hearing thee, or others of thy kind,
As full of gladness and as free of heaven,
I, with my fate contented, will plod on,
And hope for higher raptures when life's day is done.

William Wordsworth.

TO THE CUCKOO.

Hail, beauteous stranger of the grove!
  Thou messenger of Spring!
Now heaven repairs thy rural seat,
  And woods thy welcome sing.

Soon as the daisy decks the green,
  Thy certain voice we hear.
Hast thou a star to guide thy path,
  Or mark the rolling year?

Delightful visitant! with thee
  I hail the time of flowers,
And hear the sound of music sweet
  From birds among the bowers.

The school-boy, wandering through the wood
  To pull the primrose gay,
Starts, thy most curious voice to hear,
  And imitates thy lay.

What time the pea puts on the bloom,
  Thou fliest thy vocal vale,

An annual guest in other lands,
Another Spring to hail.

Sweet bird! thy bower is ever green,
Thy sky is ever clear;
Thou hast no sorrow in thy song,
No Winter in thy year!

Oh could I fly, I'd fly with thee!
We'd make, with joyful wing,
Our annual visit o'er the globe,
Attendants on the Spring.

John Logan.

TO THE CUCKOO.

O BLITHE new-comer! I have heard,
I hear thee and rejoice.
O Cuckoo! shall I call thee bird,
Or but a wandering voice?

While I am lying on the grass
Thy twofold shout I hear;
From hill to hill it seems to pass,
At once far off, and near.

Though babbling only to the vale,
Of sunshine and of flowers,
Thou bringest unto me a tale
Of visionary hours.

Thrice welcome, darling of the Spring!
E'en yet thou art to me

No bird, but an invisible thing,
  A voice, a mystery;

The same that in my school-boy days
  I listened to—that cry
Which made me look a thousand ways,
  In bush, and tree, and sky.

To seek thee did I often rove
  Through woods and on the green;
And thou wert still a hope, a love—
  Still longed for, never seen.

And I can listen to thee yet;
  Can lie upon the plain
And listen, till I do beget
  That golden time again.

O blessed bird! the earth we pace,
  Again appears to be
An unsubstantial, faery place,
  That is fit home for thee!

William Wordsworth.

THE GREEN LINNET.

Beneath these fruit-tree boughs, that shed
Their snow-white blossoms on my head,
With brightest sunshine round me spread,
  Of Spring's unclouded weather—
In this sequestered nook, how sweet
To sit upon my orchard-seat!
And birds and flowers once more to greet,
  My last year's friends together.

One have I marked, the happiest guest
In all this covert of the blest:
Hail to thee, far above the rest
In joy of voice and pinion!
Thou, Linnet! in thy green array,
Presiding spirit here to-day,
Dost lead the revels of the May,
And this is thy dominion.

While birds, and butterflies, and flowers
Make all one band of paramours,
Thou, ranging up and down the bowers,
Art sole in thy employment:
A life, a presence like the air,
Scattering thy gladness without care,
Too blest with any one to pair—
Thyself thy own enjoyment.

Amid yon tuft of hazel-trees,
That twinkle to the gusty breeze,
Behold him perched in ecstasies,
Yet seeming still to hover;
There! where the flutter of his wings
Upon his back and body flings
Shadows and sunny glimmerings,
That cover him all over.

My dazzled sight he oft deceives—
A brother of the dancing leaves—
Then flits, and from the cottage-eaves
Pours forth a song in gushes;
As if by that exulting strain

He mocked, and treated with disdain,
The voiceless form he chose to feign,
  While fluttering in the bushes.

William Wordsworth.

PIPING down the valleys wild,
  Piping songs of pleasant glee,
On a cloud I saw a child,
  And he, laughing, said to me:

"Pipe a song about a lamb."
  So I piped, with merry cheer.
"Piper, pipe that song again."
  So I piped: he wept to hear.

"Drop thy pipe, thy happy pipe,
  Sing thy songs of happy cheer."
So I sang the same again,
  While he wept with joy to hear.

"Piper, sit thee down and write,
  In a book, that all may read."—
So he vanished from my sight,
  And I plucked a hollow reed;

And I made a rural pen;
  And I stained the water clear;
And I wrote my happy songs
  Every child may joy to hear.

William Blake.

THE LAMB.

LITTLE Lamb, who made thee?
Dost thou know who made thee?
Gave thee life, and bid thee feed,
By the stream and o'er the mead;
Gave thee clothing of delight,
Softest clothing, woolly, bright;
Gave thee such a tender voice,
Making all the vales rejoice;
Little lamb, who made thee?
Dost thou know who made thee?

Little lamb, I'll tell thee;
Little lamb, I'll tell thee.
He is callèd by thy name,
For He calls Himself a Lamb.
He is meek, and He is mild,
He became a little child:
I a child, and thou a lamb,
We are callèd by His name.
Little lamb, God bless thee;
Little lamb, God bless thee!

William Blake.

VIRTUE.

SWEET day, so cool, so calm, so bright,
The bridal of the earth and sky!
The dew shall weep thy fall to-night;
For thou must die.

Sweet rose, whose hue, angry and brave,
Bids the rash gazer wipe his eye!
Thy root is ever in its grave—
And thou must die.

Sweet Spring, full of sweet days and roses,
A box where sweets compacted lie!
Thy music shows ye have your closes,
And all must die.

Only a sweet and virtuous soul,
Like seasoned timber, never gives;
But, though the whole world turn to coal,
Then chiefly lives.

George Herbert

SUMMER MORNING.

Morning again breaks through the mines of heaven,
And shakes her jewelled kirtle on the sky,
Heavy with rosy gold. Aside are driven
The vassal clouds, which bow as she draws nigh,
And catch her scattered gems of orient dye,
The pearlèd ruby which her pathway strews;
Argent and amber, now thrown useless by.
The uncolored clouds wear what she doth refuse,
For only once does Morn her sun-dyed garments use.

II.

No print of sheep-track yet hath crushed a flower;
The spider's woof with silvery dew is hung

As it was beaded ere the daylight hour:
The hookèd bramble just as it was strung,
When on each leaf the Night her crystals flung,
Then hurried off, the dawning to elude;
Before the golden-beakèd blackbird sung,
Or ere the yellow-brooms, or gorses rude,
Had bared their armèd heads in lowly gratitude.

III.

From Nature's old cathedral sweetly ring
The wild-bird choirs—burst of the woodland band,
Green-hooded Nuns, who mid the blossoms sing;
Their leafy temple, gloomy, tall, and grand,
Pillar'd with oaks, and roof'd with Heaven's own hand
Hark! how the anthem rolls through arches dun:—
"Morning again is come to light the land;
The great world's Comforter, the mighty Sun,
Hath yoked his golden steeds, the glorious race to run."

IV.

Those dusky foragers, the noisy rooks,
Have from their green high city-gates rushed out,
To rummage furrowy fields and flowery nooks;
On yonder branch now stands their glossy scout.
As yet no busy insects buzz about,
No fairy thunder o'er the air is rolled:
The drooping buds their crimson lips still pout;
Those stars of earth, the daisies white, unfold,
And soon the buttercups will give back "gold for gold."

V.

"Hark! hark! the lark" sings mid the silvery blue,
Behold her flight, proud man! and lowly bow.

She seems the first that does for pardon sue,
As though the guilty stain which lurks below
Had touched the flowers that drooped above her brow;
When she all night slept by the daisies' side;
And now she soars where purity doth flow,
Where new-born light is with no sin allied,
And, pointing with her wings, heavenward our thoughts would guide.

VI.

In belted gold the bees, with "merry march,"
Through flowery towns go sounding on their way:
They pass the red-streaked woodbine's sun-stained arch,
And onward glide through streets of sheeted May,
Nor till they reach the summer-roses stay,
Where maiden-buds are wrapt in dewy dreams,
Drowsy through breathing back the new-mown hay,
That rolls its fragrance o'er the fringèd streams—
Mirrors in which the Sun now decks his quivering beams.

VII.

Uprise the lambs, fresh from their flowery slumber
(The daisies they pressed down rise from the sod);—
He guardeth them who every star doth number,
Who called His Son a lamb—"the Lamb of God;"
And for His sake withdrew the uplifted rod,
Bidding each cloud turn to a silvery fleece,
The imaged flock for which our Shepherd trod
The paths of sorrow, that we might find peace:—
Those emblems of His love will wave till time shall cease.

VIII.

On the far sky leans the old ruined mill,
Through its rent sails the broken sunbeams glow,
Gilding the trees that belt the lower hill,
And the old thorns which on its summit grow.
Only the reedy marsh that sleeps below,
With its dwarf bushes, is concealed from view;
And now a struggling thorn its head doth show,
Another half shakes off the smoky blue,
Just where the dusty gold streams through the heavy dew:

IX.

And there the hidden river lingering dreams,
You scarce can see the banks which round it lie;
That withered trunk, a tree or shepherd seems,
Just as the light or fancy strikes the eye.
Even the very sheep, which graze hard by,
So blend their fleeces with the misty haze,
They look like clouds shook from the unsunned sky,
Ere morning o'er the eastern hills did blaze:—
The vision fades as they move farther on to graze.

X.

A checkered light streams in between the leaves,
Which on the greensward twinkle in the sun;
The deep-voiced thrush his speckled bosom heaves,
And like a silver stream his song doth run
Down the low vale, edgèd with fir-trees dun.
A little bird now hops beside the brook,
"Peaking" about like an affrighted nun;
And ever as she drinks doth upward look,
Twitters and drinks again, then seeks her cloistered nook.

XI.

What varied colors o'er the landscape play!
The very clouds seem at their ease to lean,
And the whole earth to keep glad holiday.
The lowliest bush that by the waste is seen,
Hath changed its dusky for a golden green,
In honor of this lovely Summer Morn:
The rutted roads did never seem so clean;
There is no dust upon the wayside thorn,
For every bud looks out as if but newly born.

XII.

A cottage girl trips by with side-long look,
Steadying the little basket on her head;
And where a plank bridges the narrow brook
She stops to see her fair form shadowèd.
The stream reflects her cloak of russet red;
Below she sees the trees and deep-blue sky,
The flowers which downward look in that clear bed,
The very birds which o'er its brightness fly:
She parts her loose brown hair, then wondering passes by.

XIII.

Now other forms move o'er the footpaths brown
In twos and threes; for it is Market day:
Beyond those hills stretches a little town,
And thitherward the rustics bend their way,
Crossing the scene in blue, and red, and gray;
Now by green hedge-rows, now by oak-trees old,
As they by stile or thatchèd cottage stray.
Peep through the rounded hand, and you'll behold
Such gems as Morland drew, in frames of sunny gold.

XIV.

A laden ass, a maid with wicker maun',
A shepherd lad driving his lambs to sell,
Gaudy-dressed girls move in the rosy dawn,
Women whose cloaks become the landscape well,
Farmers whose thoughts on crops and prizes dwell;
An old man with his cow and calf draws near.
Anon you hear the village carrier's bell;
Then does his gray old tilted cart appear,
Moving so slow, you think he never will get there.

XV.

They come from still green nooks, woods old and hoary,
The silent work of many a summer night,
Ere those tall trees attained their giant glory,
Or their dark tops did tower that cloudy height:
They come from spots which the gray hawthorns light,
Where stream-kissed willows make a silver shiver.
For years their steps have worn those footpaths bright
Which wind along the fields and by the river,
That makes a murmuring sound, a "ribble-bibble" ever.

XVI.

A troop of soldiers pass with stately pace—
Their early music wakes the village street:
Through yon white blinds peeps many a lovely face,
Smiling—perchance unconsciously how sweet!
One does the carpet press with blue-veined feet,
Not thinking how her fair neck she exposes,
But with white foot timing the drum's deep beat;
And, when again she on her pillow dozes,
Dreams how she'll dance that tune 'mong Summer's sweetest roses.

XVII.

So let her dream, even as beauty should!
Let the white plumes athwart her slumbers sway!
Why should I steep their swaling snow in blood,
Or bid her think of battle's grim array?
Truth will too soon her blinding star display,
And like a fearful comet meet her eyes.
And yet how peaceful they pass on their way!
How grand the sight, as up the hill they rise!—
I will not think of cities reddening in the skies.

XVIII.

How sweet those rural sounds float by the hill!
The grasshopper's shrill chirp rings o'er the ground,
The jingling sheep-bells are but seldom still,
The clapping gate closes with hollow bound,
There's music in the church-clock's measured sound.
The ring-dove's song, how breeze-like comes and goes,
Now here, now there, it seems to wander round:
The red cow's voice along the upland flows;
His bass the brindled bull from the far meadow lows.

XIX.

"Cuckoo! cuckoo!" ah! well I know thy note,
Those summer-sounds the backward years do bring,
Like Memory's locked-up bark once more afloat:
They carry me away to life's glad spring,
To home, with all its old boughs rustleing.
'Tis a sweet sound! but now I feel not glad;
I miss the voices which were wont to sing,
When on the hills I roamed a happy lad.
"Cuckoo!" it is the grave—not thou—that makes me sad.

XX.

Tell me, ye sages, whence these feelings rise—
Sorrowful mornings on the darkened soul;
Glimpses of broken, bright, and stormy skies,
O'er which this earth—the heart—has no control?
Why does the sea of thought thus backward roll?
Memory's the breeze that through the cordage raves,
And ever drives us on some homeward shoal,
As if she loved the melancholy waves
That, murmuring shoreward, break, over a reef of graves.

XXI.

Hark, how the merry bells ring o'er the vale,
Now near, remote, or lost, just as it blows.
The red cock sends his voice upon the gale;
From the thatched grange his answering rival crows:
The milkmaid o'er the dew-bathed meadow goes,
Her tucked-up kirtle ever holding tight;
And now her song rings thro' the green hedge-rows,
Her milk-kit hoops glitter like silver bright:—
I hear her lover singing somewhere out of sight.

XXII.

Where soars that spire, our rude forefathers prayed;
Thither they came, from many a thick-leaved dell,
Year after year, and o'er those footpaths strayed,
When summoned by the sounding Sabbath bell—
For in those walls they deemed that God did dwell:
And still they sleep within that bell's deep sound.
Yon spire doth here of no distinction tell;
O'er rich and poor, marble, and earthly mound,
The monument of all—it marks one common ground.

XXIII.

See yonder smoke, before it curls to heaven,
Mingles its blue amid the elm-trees tall,
Shrinking like one who fears to be forgiven;
So on the earth again doth prostrate fall,
And mid the bending green each sin recall.
Now from their beds the cottage-children rise,
Roused by some early playmate's noisy bawl;
And, on the door-step standing, rub their eyes,
Stretching their little arms, and gaping at the skies

XXIV.

The leaves "drop, drop," and dot the crispèd stream
So quick, each circle wears the first away;
Far out the tufted bulrush seems to dream,
And to the ripple nods its head alway;
The water-flags with one another play,
Bowing to every breeze that blows between
While purple dragon-flies their wings display:
The restless swallow's arrowy flight is seen,
Dimpling the sunny wave, then lost amid the green

XXV.

The boy who last night passed that darksome lane,
Trembling with every sound, and pale with fear;
Who shook when the long leaves talked to the rain,
And tried to sing, his sinking heart to cheer;
Hears now no brook wail ghost-like on his ear,
No fearful groan in the black beetle's wing;
But where the deep-dyed butterflies appear,
And on the flowers like folded pea-blooms swing,
With napless hat in hand, he after them doth spring

XXVI.

In the far sky the distant landscape melts,
Like pilèd clouds tinged with a darker hue;
Even the wood which yon high upland belts
Looks like a range of clouds, of deeper blue.
One withered tree bursts only on the view—
A bald bare oak, which on the summit grows
(And looks as if from out the sky it grew):
That tree has borne a thousand wintry snows,
And seen unnumbered mornings gild its gnarlèd boughs.

XXVII.

Yon weather-beaten gray old finger-post
Stands like Time's land-mark, pointing to decay;
The very roads it once marked out are lost:
The common was encroached on every day
By grasping men who bore an unjust sway
And rent the gift from Charity's dead hands.
That post doth still one broken arm display,
Which now points out where the new workhouse stands,
As if it said, "Poor man! those walls are all thy lands."

XXVIII.

Where o'er yon woodland-stream dark branches bow,
Patches of blue are let in from the sky,
Throwing a checkered underlight below,
Where the deep waters steeped in gloom roll by;
Looking like Hope, who ever watcheth nigh,
And throws her cheering ray o'er life's long night,
When wearied man would fain lie down and die.
Past the broad meadow now it rolleth bright,
Which like a mantle green seems edged with silver light.

XXIX.

All things, save Man, this Summer morn rejoice:
Sweet smiles the sky, so fair a world to view;
Unto the earth below the flowers give voice;
Even the wayside weed of homeliest hue
Looks up erect amid the golden blue,
And thus it speaketh to the thinking mind:—
"O'erlook me not! I for a purpose grew,
Though long mayest thou that purpose try to find:
On us one sunshine falls! God only is not blind!"

XXX.

England, my country!—land that gave me birth!
Where those I love, living or dead, still dwell,
Most sacred spot—to me—of all the earth;
England! "with all thy faults I love thee well."
With what delight I hear thy Sabbath bell
Fling to the sky its ancient English sound,
As if to the wide world it dared to tell
We own a God, who guards this envied ground,
Bulwarked with martyrs' bones—where Fear was never found.

XXXI.

Here might a sinner humbly kneel and pray,
With this bright sky, this lovely scene in view,
And worship Him who guardeth us alway!—
Who hung these lands with green, this sky with blue,
Who spake, and from these plains huge cities grew;
Who made thee, mighty England! what thou art,
And asked but gratitude for all His due.
The giver, God! claims but the beggar's part,
And only doth require "an humble, contrite heart."

Thomas Miller.

BIRDS.

OH, the sunny summer time!
Oh, the leafy summer time!
Merry is the birds' life,
When the year is in its prime!
Birds are by the water-falls,
Dashing in the rainbow spray;
Everywhere, everywhere,
Light and lovely things are they!
Birds are in the forest old,
Building in each hoary tree;
Birds are on the green hills,
Birds are on the sea!

On the moor and in the fen,
'Mong the whortleberries green,
In the yellow furze-bush
There the joyous bird is seen;
In the heather on the hill,
All among the mountain thyme;
By the little brooksides,
Where the sparkling waters chime;
In the crag, and on the peak,
Splintered, savage, wild, and bare,
There the bird with wild wings
Wheeleth through the air.

Wheeleth through the breezy air,
Singing, screaming in his flight,

Calling to his bird-mate,
  In troubleless delight!
In the green and leafy wood,
  Where the branching ferns upcurl,
Soon as is the dawning
  Wake the mavis and the merle;
Wakes the cuckoo on the bough,
  Wakes the jay with ruddy breast,
Wakes the mother ring-dove,
  Brooding on her nest!

Oh, the sunny summer time!
  Oh, the leafy summer time!
Merry is the birds' life,
  When the year is in its prime!
Some are strong, and some are weak,
  Some love day, and some love night,
But whate'er a bird is,
  Whate'er loves—it has delight
In the joyous song it sings,
  In the liquid air it cleaves,
In the sunshine, in the shower,
  In the nest it weaves.

Do we wake, or do we sleep,
  Go our fancies in a crowd,
After many a dull care,
  Birds are singing loud!
Sing then, linnet, sing then, wren,
  Merle and mavis, sing your fill;
And thou, rapturous skylark,
  Sing and soar up from the hill!

Sing, O nightingale, and pour
  Out for us sweet fancies new;
Singing for us, birds,
  We will sing of you!

Mary Howitt.

THE THRUSH'S NEST.

Within a thick and spreading hawthorn bush
  That overhung a molehill large and round,
I heard from morn to morn a merry thrush
  Sing hymns of rapture, while I drank the sound
With joy—and oft, an unintruding guest,
  I watched her secret toils from day to day;
How true she warped the moss to form her nest,
  And modelled it within with wood and clay.
And by and by, like heath-bells gilt with dew,
  There lay her shining eggs as bright as flowers,
Ink-spotted over, shells of green and blue;
  And there I witnessed, in the summer hours,
A brood of nature's minstrels chirp and fly,
Glad as the sunshine and the laughing sky.

John Clare.

TO THE RED-BREAST.

When that the fields put on their gay attire,
  Thou silent sitt'st near brake or river's brim,
Whilst the gay thrush sings loud from covert dim;
  But when pale Winter lights the social fire,

And meads with slime are sprent and ways with mire,
  Thou charm'st us with thy soft and solemn hymn,
  From battlement, or barn, or hay-stack trim;
And now not seldom turn'st, as if for hire,
  Thy thrilling pipe to me, waiting to catch
The pittance due to thy well-warbled song;
  Sweet bird, sing on! for oft near lonely hatch,
Like thee, myself have pleased the rustic throng,
  And oft for entrance, 'neath the peaceful thatch,
Full many a tale have told and ditty long.

John Bampfylde.

THE GRASSHOPPER.

Happy insect, what can be
In happiness compared to thee?
Fed with nourishment divine,
The dewy morning's gentle wine!
Nature waits upon thee still,
And thy verdant cup does fill;
'Tis filled wherever thou dost tread,
Nature's self's thy Ganymede.
Thou dost drink, and dance, and sing,
Happier than the happiest king!
All the fields which thou dost see,
All the plants belong to thee;
All that summer hours produce,
Fertile made with early juice.
Man for thee does sow and plough;
Farmer he, and landlord thou!
Thou dost innocently enjoy;
Nor does thy luxury destroy.

The shepherd gladly heareth thee,
More harmonious than he.
Thee country hinds with gladness hear,
Prophet of the ripened year!
Thee Phœbus loves, and does inspire;
Phœbus is himself thy sire.
To thee, of all things upon earth,
Life is no longer than thy mirth.
Happy insect! happy thou,
Dost neither age nor winter know;
But when thou'st drunk, and danced, and sung
Thy fill, the flowery leaves among
(Voluptuous and wise withal,
Epicurean animal!),
Sated with thy summer feast,
Thou retir'st to endless rest.

Abraham Cowley.

THE GRASSHOPPER AND CRICKET.

GREEN little vaulter in the sunny grass,
Catching your heart up at the feel of June—
Sole voice that's heard amidst the lazy noon,
When even the bees lag at the summoning brass;
And you, warm little housekeeper, who class
With those who think the candles come too soon,
Loving the fire, and with your tricksome tune
Nick the glad silent moments as they pass!

O sweet and tiny cousins, that belong,
One to the fields, the other to the hearth,

Both have your sunshine; both, though small, are strong
  At your clear hearts; and both seem given to earth
To sing in thoughtful ears this natural song—
  In doors and out, summer and winter, mirth.

Leigh Hunt.

ON THE GRASSHOPPER AND CRICKET.

The poetry of earth is never dead:
  When all the birds are faint with the hot sun,
  And hide in cooling trees, a voice will run
From hedge to hedge about the new-mown mead.
That is the Grasshopper's—he takes the lead
  In summer luxury—he has never done
  With his delights; for, when tired out with fun,
He rests at ease beneath some pleasant weed.
  The poetry of earth is ceasing never.
On a lone winter evening, when the frost
Has wrought a silence, from the stove there shrills
  The Cricket's song, in warmth increasing ever,
And seems, to one in drowsiness half lost,
The Grasshopper's among some grassy hills.

John Keats.

TO A BEE.

Thou wert out betimes, thou busy, busy Bee!
    As abroad I took my early way,
  Before the cow from her resting-place
  Had risen up and left her trace

On the meadow, with dew so gray,
Saw I thee, thou busy, busy Bee.

Thou wert working late, thou busy, busy Bee!
After the fall of the cistus flower;
When the primrose of evening was ready to burst,
I heard thee last as I saw thee first;
In the silence of the evening hour,
Heard I thee, thou busy, busy Bee.

Thou art a miser, thou busy, busy Bee!
Late and early at employ;
Still on thy golden stores intent,
Thy summer in heaping and hoarding is spent
What thy winter will never enjoy;
Wise lesson this for me, thou busy, busy Bee.

Little dost thou think, thou busy, busy Bee!
What is the end of thy toil.
When the latest flowers of the ivy are gone,
And all thy work for the year is done,
Thy master comes for the spoil:
Woe then for thee, thou busy, busy Bee!

Robert Southey.

TO A BUTTERFLY.

Stay near me; do not take thy flight!
A little longer stay in sight!
Much converse do I find in thee,
Historian of my infancy!

Float near me; do not yet depart!
  Dead times revive in thee,
Thou bring'st, gay creature as thou art!
A solemn image to my heart,
  My father's family!

Oh! pleasant, pleasant were the days,
The time when, in our childish plays,
My sister Emeline and I
Together chased the butterfly!
A very hunter did I rush
  Upon the prey:—with leaps and springs
I followed on from brake to bush;
But she, God love her! feared to brush
  The dust from off its wings.

William Wordsworth.

TO THE CICADA.

CICADA! drunk with drops of dew,
What musician equals you,
In the shady solitude?
On a perch amidst the wood,
Scraping to your heart's desire
Dusky sides with notchy feet,
Shrilling, thrilling, fast and sweet,
Like the music of a lyre.
Dear Cicada! I entreat,
Sing the Dryads something new;
So from thick-embowered seat,
Pan himself may answer you.

Till every inmost glade rejoices
With your loud alternate voices:
And I listen, and forget
All the thorns, the doubts and fears,
Love in lover's heart may set;
Listen, and forget them all.
And so, with music in mine ears,
Where the plane-tree shadows steep
The ground with coldness, softly fall
Into a noontide sleep.

William Allingham.

THE WATERFALL.

When the fir-tree dreams in the drowsy haze
  Of the motionless August hour;
When even the eagle-leafed aspen droops,
  And asleep is the bird in its bower;
Wakeful alone sends the Waterfall then
  Its mellow melodious hum,
Wafting a coolness where all is heat,
  And music where all is dumb.

In the bloomy May, when the buoyant day
  Is breezy and sunny and glad;
When the lithe bough sweeps and the swift brooks leap,
  And the birds sing and soar as if mad;
Amid this orchestral blithesomeness,
  This pæan of Spring-time's reign,
The Waterfall's bound fills the scene all round
  With its blending, exulting strain.

In its crannies the hair-stemmed columbine nods,
  The fern in its sprinkles drips;
And the little black dipper all over the bridge
  Of the spanning pine-tree skips.
And the bubbles they toss on the smitten gloss
  Of the dashing and flashing pool;
Where the angler scoops up his wreathed hopple-leaf cup,
  And the trout poises deep in the cool.

Alfred B. Street.

SONG OF THE SUMMER WINDS.

Up the dale and down the bourne,
  O'er the meadow swift we fly;
Now we sing, and now we mourn,
  Now we whistle, now we sigh.

By the grassy-fringed river,
  Through the murmuring reeds we sweep;
Mid the lily-leaves we quiver,
  To their very hearts we creep.

Now the maiden rose is blushing
  At the frolic things we say,
While aside her cheek we're rushing,
  Like some truant bees at play.

Through the blooming groves we rustle,
  Kissing every bud we pass,—
As we did it in the bustle,
  Scarcely knowing how it was.

Down the glen, across the mountain,
  O'er the yellow heath we roam,
Whirling round about the fountain,
  Till its little breakers foam.

Bending down the weeping willows,
  While our vesper hymn we sigh;
Then unto our rosy pillows
  On our weary wings we hie.

There, of idlenesses dreaming,
  Scarce from waking we refrain,
Moments long as ages deeming
  Till we're at our play again.

George Darley.

THEY COME! THE MERRY SUMMER MONTHS.

They come! the merry summer months of beauty, song,
  and flowers;
They come! the gladsome months that bring thick leafi-
  ness to bowers.
Up, up, my heart! and walk abroad; fling cark and care
  aside;
Seek silent hills, or rest thyself where peaceful waters
  glide;
Or, underneath the shadow vast of patriarchal tree,
Scan through its leaves the cloudless sky in rapt tran-
  quillity.

The grass is soft, its velvet touch is grateful to the
hand;
And, like the kiss of maiden love, the breeze is sweet
and bland;
The daisy and the buttercup are nodding courteously;
It stirs their blood with kindest love, to bless and wel-
come thee:
And mark how with thy own thin locks—they now are
silvery gray—
That blissful breeze is wantoning, and whispering, "Be
gay!"

There is no cloud that sails along the ocean of yon
sky,
But hath its own winged mariners to give it melody:
Thou seest their glittering fans outspread, all gleaming
like red gold;
And hark! with shrill pipe musical, their merry course
they hold.
God bless them all, those little ones, who, far above this
earth,
Can make a scoff of its mean joys, and vent a nobler
mirth.

But soft! mine ear upcaught a sound—from yonder
wood it came!
The spirit of the dim green glade did breathe his own
glad name;
Yes, it is he! the hermit bird, that, apart from all his
kind,
Slow spells his beads monotonous to the soft western
wind;

Cuckoo! Cuckoo! he sings again—his notes are void of
art;
But simplest strains do soonest sound the deep founts of
the heart.

Good Lord! it is a gracious boon for thought-crazed
wight like me,
To smell again these summer flowers beneath this sum-
mer tree!
To suck once more in every breath their little souls away,
And feed my fancy with fond dreams of youth's bright
summer day,
When, rushing forth like untamed colt, the reckless,
truant boy,
Wandered through greenwoods all day long, a mighty
heart of joy!

I'm sadder now—I have had cause; but oh! I'm proud
to think
That each pure joy-fount, loved of yore, I yet delight to
drink;
Leaf, blossom, blade, hill, valley, stream, the calm, un-
clouded sky,
Still mingle music with my dreams, as in the days gone
by,
When summer's loveliness and light fall round me dark
and cold,
I'll bear indeed life's heaviest curse,—a heart that hath
waxed old!

William Motherwell.

UNWATCHED the garden bough shall sway,
  The tender blossom flutter down,
  Unloved that beech will gather brown,
This maple burn itself away;

Unloved the sunflower, shining fair,
  Ray round with flames her disk of seed,
  And many a rose-carnation feed
With summer spice the humming air;

Unloved by many a sandy bar,
  The brook shall babble down the plain,
  At noon, or when the lesser wain
Is twisting round the polar star;

Uncared for, gird the windy grove,
  And flood the haunts of hern and crake;
  Or into silvery arrows break
The sailing moon in creek and cove;

Till from the garden and the wild
  A fresh association blow,
  And year by year the landscape grow
Familiar to the stranger's child;

As year by year the laborer tills
  His wonted glebe, or lops the glades;
  And year by year our memory fades
From all the circle of the hills.

Alfred Tennyson.

THE PRAISE OF A COUNTRYMAN'S LIFE.

Oh, the sweet contentment
The countryman doth find!
Heigh trolollie, lollie, lol, heigh trolollie, lee;
That quiet contemplation
Possesseth all my mind;
Then, care away, and wend along with me.

For courts are full of flattery,
As hath too oft been tried;
Heigh trolollie, lollie, lol, heigh trolollie, lee;
The city full of wantonness,
And both are full of pride;
Then, care away, and wend along with me.

But, oh! the honest countryman
Speaks truly from his heart;
Heigh trolollie, lollie, lol, heigh trolollie, lee;
His pride is in his tillage,
His horses, and his cart;
Then, care away, and wend along with me.

Our clothing is good sheepskins,
Gray russet for our wives;
Heigh trolollie, lollie, lol, heigh trolollie, lee;
'Tis warmth, and not gay clothing,
That doth prolong our lives;
Then, care away, and wend along with me.

The ploughman, though he labor hard,
Yet on the holy day,
Heigh trolollie, lollie, lol, heigh trolollie, lee;
No emperor so merrily
Does pass his time away;
Then, care away, and wend along with me.

To recompense our tillage,
The heavens afford us showers,
Heigh trolollie, lollie, lol, heigh trolollie, lee;
And for our sweet refreshments
The earth affords us bowers;
Then, care away, and wend along with me.

The cuckoo and the nightingale
Full merrily do sing,
Heigh trolollie, lollie, lol, heigh trolollie, lee;
And with their pleasant roundelays
Do welcome in the spring;
Then, care away, and wend along with me.

This is not half the happiness
The countryman enjoys;
Heigh trolollie, lollie, lol, heigh trolollie, lee;
Though others think they have as much,
Yet he that says so lies;
Then, care away, and come along with me.

John Chalkhill.

THE WILD CHERRY-TREE.

OH, there never was yet so fair a thing,
By racing river or bubbling spring,
Nothing that ever so gayly grew
Up from the ground when the skies were blue,
Nothing so brave, nothing so free,
As *thou*, my wild, wild Cherry-tree!

Jove! how it danced in the gusty breeze!
Jove! how it frolicked amongst the trees!
Dashing the pride of the poplar down,
Stripping the thorn of his hoary crown!
Oak or ash—what matter to *thee?*
'Twas the same to my wild, wild Cherry-tree.

Never at rest, like one that's young,
Abroad to the winds its arms it flung,
Shaking its bright and crownèd head,
Whilst I stole up for its berries red.
Beautiful berries! beautiful tree!
Hurrah! for the wild, wild Cherry-tree!

Back I fly to the days gone by,
And I see thy branches against the sky;
I see on the grass thy blossoms dead,
I see (nay, I taste) thy berries red,
And I shout like the tempest, loud and free,
Hurrah! for the wild, wild Cherry-tree!

Barry Cornwall.

THE GARDEN.

How vainly men themselves amaze,
To win the palm, the oak, or bays,
And their incessant labors see
Crowned from some single herb or tree,
Whose short and narrow-vergèd shade
Does prudently their toils upbraid!
While all the flowers and trees do close,
To weave the garlands of repose.

Fair Quiet, have I found thee here,
And Innocence, thy sister dear?
Mistaken long, I sought you then
In busy companies of men.
Your sacred plants, if here below,
Only among the plants will grow;
Society is all but rude
To this delicious solitude.

No white nor red was ever seen
So amorous as this lovely green.
Fond lovers, cruel as their flame,
Cut in these trees their mistress' name;
Little, alas! they know or heed,
How far these beauties her exceed!
Fair trees! where'er your barks I wound,
No name shall but your own be found.

When we have run our passion's heat.
Love hither makes his best retreat.

The gods, who mortal beauty chase,
Still in a tree did end their race.
Apollo hunted Daphne so,
Only that she might laurel grow;
And Pan did after Syrinx speed,
Not as a nymph, but for a reed.

What wondrous life is this I lead!
Ripe apples drop about my head;
The luscious clusters of the vine
Upon my mouth do crush their wine;
The nectarine, and curious peach,
Into my hands themselves do reach;
Stumbling on melons, as I pass,
Insnared with flowers, I fall on grass.

Meanwhile the mind from pleasure less
Withdraws into its happiness:
The mind, that ocean where each kind
Does straight its own resemblance find;
Yet it creates, transcending these,
Far other worlds and other seas;
Annihilating all that's made
To a green thought in a green shade.

Here at the fountain's sliding foot,
Or at some fruit-tree's mossy root,
Casting the body's vest aside,
My soul into the boughs does glide;
There, like a bird, it sits and sings,
Then whets and claps its silver wings,
And, till prepared for longer flight,
Waves in its plumes the various light.

Such was the happy garden state,
While man there walked without a mate:
After a place so pure and sweet,
What other help could yet be meet!
But 'twas beyond a mortal's share
To wander solitary there:
Two paradises are in one,
To live in paradise alone.

How well the skilful gard'ner drew
Of flowers, and herbs, this dial new!
Where from above the milder sun
Does through a fragrant zodiac run:
And, as it works, th' industrious bee
Computes its time as well as we.
How could such sweet and wholesome hours
Be reckoned, but with herbs and flowers?

Andrew Marvell.

SONG.

HAYMAKERS, rakers, reapers, and mowers,
Wait on your Summer-queen;
Dress up with musk-rose her eglantine bowers,
Daffodils strew the green:
Sing, dance, and play,
'Tis holiday:
The Sun does bravely shine
On our ears of corn.
Rich as a pearl
Comes every girl:

This is mine, this is mine, this is mine!
Let us die ere away they be borne.

Bow to the Sun, to our queen, and that fair one
Come to behold our sports:
Each bonny lass here is counted a rare one,
As those in a prince's courts.
These and we,
With country glee,
Will teach the woods to resound,
And the hills with echoes hollow;
Skipping lambs
Their bleating dams,
'Mongst kids shall trip it round;
For joy thus our wenches we follow.

Wind, jolly huntsmen, your neat bugles shrilly,
Hounds, make a lusty cry;
Spring up, you falconers, the partridges freely,
Then let your brave hawks fly.
Horses amain,
Over ridge, over plain,
The dogs have the stag in chase:
'Tis a sport to content a king.
So, ho, ho! through the skies
How the proud bird flies,
And sousing, kills with a grace!
Now the deer falls: hark, how they ring!

John Ford.

NOON.

All how silent and how still;
Nothing heard but yonder mill:
While the dazzled eye surveys
All around a liquid blaze;
And amid the scorching gleams,
If we earnest look, it seems
As if crooked bits of glass
Seemed repeatedly to pass.
Oh, for a puffing breeze to blow!
But breezes are all strangers now;
Not a twig is seen to shake,
Nor the smallest bent to quake;
From the river's muddy side
Not a curve is seen to glide;
And no longer on the stream,
Watching, lies the silver bream,
Forcing, from repeated springs,
"Verges in successive rings."
Bees are faint, and cease to hum;
Birds are overpowered and dumb.
Rural voices all are mute,
Tuneless lie the pipe and flute;
Shepherds, with their panting sheep,
In the swaliest corner creep;
And from the tormenting heat
All are wishing to retreat.
Huddled up in grass and flowers,
Mowers wait for cooler hours;

And the cow-boy seeks the sedge,
Romping in the woodland hedge,
While his cattle o'er the vales
Scamper, with uplifted tails;
Others, not so wild and mad,
That can better bear the gad,
Underneath the hedge-row lunge,
Or, if nigh, in waters plunge.
Oh! to see how flowers are took,
How it grieves me when I look;
Ragged-robins, once so pink,
Now are turned as black as ink,
And the leaves, being scorched so much,
Even crumble at the touch;
Drowking lies the meadow-sweet,
Flopping down beneath one's feet:
While to all the flowers that blow,
If in open air they grow,
Th' injurious deed alike is done
By the hot, relentless sun.
E'en the dew is parchèd up
From the teasel's jointed cup:
O poor birds! where must ye fly,
Now your water-pots are dry?
If ye stay upon the heath,
Ye'll be choaked and clammed to death:
Therefore leave the shadeless goss,
Seek the spring-head lined with moss;
There your little feet may stand,
Safely printing on the sand;
While, in full possession, where
Purling eddies ripple clear,

You, with ease and plenty blest,
Sip the coolest and the best.
Then away! and wet your throats;
Cheer me with your warbling notes;
'Twill hot noon the more revive;
While I wander to contrive
For myself a place as good,
In the middle of a wood:
There, aside some mossy bank,
Where the grass, in bunches rank,
Lifts its down on spindles high,
Shall be where I'll choose to lie;
Fearless of the things that creep,
Then I'll think, and then I'll sleep;
Caring not to stir at all,
Till the dew begins to fall.

John Clare.

TO A RED CLOVER BLOSSOM.

Sweet bottle-shaped flower of lushy red,
  Born when the summer wakes her warmest breeze,
Among the meadow's waving grasses spread,
  Or 'neath the shade of hedge or clumping trees,
Bowing on slender stem thy heavy head,
  In sweet delight I view thy summer bed,
And list the drone of heavy humblebees
  Along thy honeyed garden gayly led,
Down corn-fields, striped balks, and pasture-leas.
  Fond warmings of the soul, that long have fled,

Revive my bosom with their kindlings still,
  As I bend musing o'er thy ruddy pride;
Recalling days when, dropt upon a hill,
  I cut my oaten trumpets by thy side.

John Clare.

THE BRAMBLE FLOWER.

Thy fruit full well the schoolboy knows,
  Wild bramble of the brake!
So, put thou forth thy small white rose;
  I love it for his sake.
Though woodbines flaunt and roses glow
  O'er all the fragrant bowers,
Thou need'st not be ashamed to show
  Thy satin-threaded flowers;

For dull the eye, the heart is dull,
  That cannot feel how fair,
Amid all beauty beautiful,
  Thy tender blossoms are;
How delicate thy gauzy frill,
  How rich thy branchy stem,
How soft thy voice when woods are still
  And thou sing'st hymns to them;

While silent showers are falling slow,
  And, mid the general hush,
A sweet air lifts the little bough,
  Lone whispering through the bush!
The primrose to the grave is gone;
  The hawthorn flower is dead;

The violet by the mossed gray stone
  Hath laid her weary head;

But thou! wild bramble! back dost bring,
  In all their beauteous power,
The fresh green days of life's fair Spring,
  And boyhood's blossomy hour.
Scornèd bramble of the brake! once more
  Thou bidd'st me be a boy,
To gad with thee the woodlands o'er,
  In freedom and in joy.

Ebenezer Elliott.

A PASTORAL SONG.

Hither! hither!
O come hither!
Lads and lasses, come and see!
Trip it neatly,
Foot it featly,
O'er the grassy turf to me!

Here are bowers
Hung with flowers,
Richly curtain'd halls for you!
Meads for rovers,
Shades for lovers,
Violet beds, and pillows too!

Purple heather
You may gather
Sandal-deep in seas of bloom,

Pale-faced lily,
Proud Sweet-Willy,
Gorgeous rose, and golden broom!

Odorous blossoms
For sweet bosoms,
Garlands green to bind the hair;
Crowns and kirtles,
Weft of myrtles,
Youth may choose, and Beauty wear!

Brightsome glasses
For bright faces
'Shine in ev'ry rill that flows;
Every minute
You look in it
Still more bright your beauty grows!

Banks for sleeping,
Nooks for peeping,
Glades for dancing, smooth and fine!
Fruits delicious
For who wishes,
Nectar, dew, and honey-wine!

Hither! hither!
O come hither!
Lads and lasses, come and see!
Trip it neatly,
Foot it featly,
O'er the grassy turf to me!

George Darley.

A SERENADE.

AWAKE thee, my Lady-love!
Wake thee, and rise!
The sun through the bower peeps
Into thine eyes!

Behold how the early lark
Springs from the corn!
Hark, hark how the flower-bird
Winds her wee horn!

The swallow's glad shriek is heard
All through the air!
The stock-dove is murmuring
Loud as she dare!

Apollo's winged bugleman
Cannot contain,
But peals his loud trumpet-call
Once and again!

Then wake thee, my Lady-love!
Bird of my bower!
The sweetest and sleepiest
Bird at this hour!

George Darley.

A SCENE.

THE Landscape's stretching view, that opens wide,
With dribbling brooks, and river's wider floods,
And hills, and vales, and darksome lowering woods,
With green of varied hues, and grasses pied;

The low brown cottage in the sheltered nook;
The steeple, peeping just above the trees
Whose dangling leaves keep rustling in the breeze;
And thoughtful shepherd bending o'er his hook;
And maidens stripped, haymaking too, appear;
And Hodge a-whistling at his fallow plough;
And herdsmen hallooing to intruding cow:
All these, with hundreds more, far off or near,
Approach my sight; and please to such excess,
That language fails the pleasure to express.

John Clare.

A LAIR AT NOON.

The hawthorn gently stopped the sun, beneath,
The ash above its quivering shadows spread,
And downy bents, that to the air did wreathe,
Bowed 'neath my pressure in an easy bed:
The water whirlèd round each stunted nook,
And sweet the splashings on the ear did swim,
Of fly-bit cattle gulching in the brook,
Nibbling the grasses on the fountain's brim:
The little minnows, driven from their retreat,
Still sought the shelving bank to shun the heat.
I fain had slept, but flies would buzz around;
I fain had lookèd calmly on the scene,
But the sweet snug retreat my search had found
Wakened the Muse to sing the woody screen.

John Clare.

The Summer, the divinest Summer burns,
  The skies are bright with azure and with gold;
The mavis and the nightingale, by turns,
  Amid the woods a soft enchantment hold:
The flowering woods, with glory and delight,
  Their tender leaves unto the air have spread;
The wanton air, amid their alleys bright,
  Doth softly fly, and a light fragrance shed:
The nymphs within the silver fountains play,
  The angels on the golden banks recline,
Wherein great Flora, in her bright array,
  Hath sprinkled her ambrosial sweets divine:
Or, else, I gaze upon that beauteous face,
O Amoret! and think these sweets have place!

Lord Thurlow.

A SUMMER RAMBLE.

The quiet August noon has come,
  A slumberous silence fills the sky;
The fields are still, the woods are dumb,
  In glassy sleep the waters lie.

And mark yon soft white clouds that rest
  Above our vale, a moveless throng;
The cattle, on the mountain's breast,
  Enjoy the grateful shadow long.

Oh, how unlike those merry hours
  In early June, when Earth laughs out,
When the fresh winds make love to flowers,
  And woodlands sing and waters shout!

When in the grass sweet voices talk,
  And strains of tiny music swell
From every moss-cup of the rock,
  From every nameless blossom's bell.

But now a joy too deep for sound,
  A peace no other season knows,
Hushes the heavens and wraps the ground,
  The blessing of supreme repose.

Away! I will not be, to-day,
  The only slave of toil and care.
Away from desk and dust! away!
  I'll be as idle as the air.

Beneath the open sky abroad,
  Among the plants and breathing things,
The sinless, peaceful works of God,
  I'll share the calm the season brings.

Come thou, in whose soft eyes I see
  The gentle meanings of thy heart,
One day amid the woods with me,
  From men and all their cares apart.

And where, upon the meadow's breast,
  The shadow of the thicket lies,
The blue wild flowers thou gatherest
  Shall glow yet deeper near thine eyes.

Come, and when, mid the calm profound,
  I turn, those gentle eyes to seek,
They, like the lovely landscape round,
  Of innocence and peace shall speak.

Rest here, beneath the unmoving shade,
  And on the silent valleys gaze,
Winding and widening, till they fade
  In yon soft ring of summer haze.

The village trees their summits rear,
  Still as its spire, and yonder flock
At rest in those calm fields appear
  As chiselled from the lifeless rock.

One tranquil mount the scene o'erlooks—
  There the hushed winds their sabbath keep,
While a near hum from bees and brooks
  Comes faintly, like the breath of sleep.

Well may the gazer deem that when,
  Worn with the struggle and the strife,
And heart-sick at the wrongs of men,
  The good forsakes the scene of life;

Like this deep quiet that, awhile,
  Lingers the lovely landscape o'er,
Shall be the peace whose holy smile
  Welcomes him to a happier shore.

William Cullen Bryant.

A WISH.

Mine be a cot beside the hill:
  A bee-hive's hum shall soothe my ear·
A willowy brook, that turns a mill,
  With many a fall shall linger near.

The swallow oft beneath my thatch
  Shall twitter from her clay-built nest;
Oft shall the pilgrim lift the latch,
  And share my meal, a welcome guest.

Around my ivied porch shall spring
  Each fragrant flower that drinks the dew;
And Lucy, at her wheel, shall sing
  In russet gown and apron blue.

The village-church among the trees,
  Where first our marriage-vows were given,
With merry peals shall swell the breeze,
  And point with taper spire to heaven.

Samuel Rogers.

GRONGAR HILL.

Silent nymph, with curious eye!
Who, the purple evening, lie
On the mountain's lonely van,
Beyond the noise of busy man—
Painting fair the form of things,
While the yellow linnet sings,

Or the tuneful nightingale
Charms the forest with her tale—
Come, with all thy various hues,
Come, and aid thy sister Muse.
Now, while Phœbus, riding high,
Gives lustre to the land and sky,
Grongar Hill invites my song—
Draw the landscape bright and strong;
Grongar, in whose mossy cells
Sweetly musing Quiet dwells;
Grongar, in whose silent shade,
For the modest Muses made,
So oft I have, the evening still,
At the fountain of a rill,
Sat upon a flowery bed,
With my hand beneath my head,
While strayed my eyes o'er Towy's flood,
Over mead and over wood,
From house to house, from hill to hill,
Till Contemplation had her fill.
About his checkered sides I wind,
And leave his brooks and meads behind,
And groves and grottoes where I lay,
And vistas shooting beams of day.
Wide and wider spreads the vale,
As circles on a smooth canal.
The mountains round, unhappy fate!
Sooner or later, of all height,
Withdraw their summits from the skies,
And lessen as the others rise.
Still the prospect wider spreads,
Adds a thousand woods and meads;

Still it widens, widens still,
And sinks the newly-risen hill.
Now I gain the mountain's brow;
What a landscape lies below!
No clouds, no vapors intervene;
But the gay, the open scene
Does the face of Nature show
In all the hues of heaven's bow!
And, swelling to embrace the light,
Spreads around beneath the sight.
Old castles on the cliffs arise,
Proudly tow'ring in the skies;
Rushing from the woods, the spires
Seem from hence ascending fires;
Half his beams Apollo sheds
On the yellow mountain-heads,
Gilds the fleeces of the flocks,
And glitters on the broken rocks.
Below me trees unnumbered rise,
Beautiful in various dyes:
The gloomy pine, the poplar blue,
The yellow beech, the sable yew,
The slender fir that taper grows,
The sturdy oak with broad-spread boughs;
And beyond, the purple grove,
Haunt of Phyllis, queen of Love!
Gaudy as the opening dawn,
Lies a long and level lawn,
On which a dark hill, steep and high,
Holds and charms the wandering eye;
Deep are his feet in Towy's flood:
His sides are clothed with waving wood;

And ancient towers crown his brow,
That cast an awful look below;
Whose ragged walls the ivy creeps,
And with her arms from falling keeps;
So both, a safety from the wind
In mutual dependence find.
'Tis now the raven's bleak abode;
'Tis now th' apartment of the toad;
And there the fox securely feeds;
And there the poisonous adder breeds,
Concealed in ruins, moss, and weeds;
While, ever and anon, there fall
Huge heaps of hoary, mouldered wall.
Yet Time has seen—that lifts the low
And level lays the lofty brow—
Has seen this broken pile complete,
Big with the vanity of state.
But transient is the smile of Fate!
A little rule, a little sway,
A sunbeam in a winter's day,
Is all the proud and mighty have
Between the cradle and the grave.
And see the rivers, how they run
Through woods and meads, in shade and sun,
Sometimes swift, sometimes slow—
Wave succeeding wave, they go
A various journey to the deep,
Like human life to endless sleep!
Thus is Nature's vesture wrought
To instruct our wandering thought;
Thus she dresses green and gay
To disperse our cares away.

Ever charming, ever new,
When will the landscape tire the view!
The fountain's fall, the river's flow;
The woody valleys, warm and low;
The windy summit, wild and high,
Roughly rushing on the sky;
The pleasant seat, the ruined tower,
The naked rock, the shady bower;
The town and village, dome and farm—
Each gives each a double charm,
As pearls upon an Ethiop's arm.
See on the mountain's southern side,
Where the prospect opens wide,
Where the evening gilds the tide,
How close and small the hedges lie;
What streaks of meadow cross the eye!
A step, methinks, may pass the stream,
So little distant dangers seem;
So we mistake the Future's face,
Eyed through Hope's deluding glass;
As yon summits, soft and fair,
Clad in colors of the air,
Which, to those who journey near,
Barren, brown, and rough appear;
Still we tread the same coarse way—
The present's still a cloudy day.
O may I with myself agree,
And never covet what I see;
Content me with an humble shade,
My passions tamed, my wishes laid;
For while our wishes wildly roll,
We banish quiet from the soul.

'Tis thus the busy beat the air,
And misers gather wealth and care.
  Now, even now, my joys run high,
As on the mountain turf I lie;
While the wanton Zephyr sings,
And in the vale perfumes his wings;
While the waters murmur deep;
While the shepherd charms his sheep;
While the birds unbounded fly,
And with music fill the sky,
Now, even now, my joys run high.
  Be full, ye courts; be great who will;
Search for Peace with all your skill;
Open wide the lofty door,
Seek her on the marble floor.
In vain you search; she is not here!
In vain you search the domes of Care!
Grass and flowers Quiet treads,
On the meads and mountain-heads,
Along with Pleasure—close allied,
Ever by each other's side;
And often, by the murmuring rill,
Hears the thrush, while all is still
Within the groves of Grongar Hill.

John Dyder.

THE HAMLET.

The hinds how blest, who, ne'er beguiled
To quit their hamlet's hawthorn wild,
Nor haunt the crowd, nor tempt the main,
For splendid care, and guilty gain!

When morning's twilight-cinctured beam
Strikes their low thatch with slanting gleam,
They rove abroad in ether blue,
To dip the scythe in fragrant dew;
The sheaf to bind, the beech to fell,
That nodding shades a craggy dell.

Midst gloomy glades, in warbles clear,
Wild nature's sweetest notes they hear;
On green, untrodden banks they view
The hyacinth's neglected hue:
In their lone haunts, and woodland rounds,
They spy the squirrel's airy bounds;
And startle from her ashen spray
Across the glen the screaming jay;
Each native charm their steps explore
Of Solitude's sequestered shore.

For them the moon with cloudless ray
Mounts to illume their homeward way:
Their weary spirits to relieve,
The meadows incense breathe at eve.
No riot mars the simple fare,
That o'er a glimmering hearth they share:
But when the curfew's measured roar
Duly, the darkening valleys o'er,
Has echoed from the distant town,
They wish no beds of cygnet-down,
No trophied canopies, to close
Their drooping eyes in quick repose.

Their little sons, who spread the bloom
Of health around the clay-built room,

Or through the primrosed coppice stray,
Or gambol on the new-mown hay;
Or quaintly braid the cowslip twine,
Or drive afield the tardy kine;
Or hasten from the sultry hill,
To loiter at the shady rill;
Or climb the tall pine's gloomy crest,
To rob the raven's ancient nest.

Their humble porch with honeyed flowers
The curling woodbine's shade embowers:
From the small garden's thymy mound
Their bees in busy swarms resound:
Nor fell disease before his time
Hastes to consume life's golden prime:
But when their temples long have wore
The silver crown of tresses hoar,
As studious still calm peace to keep,
Beneath a flowery turf they sleep.

Joseph Warton.

THE EVENING WIND.

Spirit that breathest through my lattice! thou
That cool'st the twilight of the sultry day!
Gratefully flows thy freshness round my brow;
Thou hast been out upon the deep at play,
Riding all day the wild blue waves till now,
Roughening their crests, and scattering high their spray,
And swelling the white sail. I welcome thee
To the scorched land, thou wanderer of the sea!

Nor I alone—a thousand bosoms round
  Inhale thee in the fulness of delight;
And languid forms rise up, and pulses bound
  Livelier, at coming of the wind of night;
And languishing to hear thy welcome sound
  Lies the vast inland, stretched beyond the sight.
Go forth into the gathering shade; go forth—
God's blessing breathed upon the fainting earth!

Go, rock the little wood-bird in his nest;
  Curl the still waters, bright with stars; and rouse
The wide old wood from his majestic rest,
  Summoning, from the innumerable boughs,
The strange deep harmonies that haunt his breast.
  Pleasant shall be thy way where meekly bows
The shutting flower, and darkling waters pass,
And where the o'ershadowing branches sweep the grass.

Stoop o'er the place of graves, and softly sway
  The sighing herbage by the gleaming stone;
That they who near the churchyard willows stray,
  And listen in the deepening gloom, alone,
May think of gentle souls that passed away,
  Like thy pure breath, into the vast unknown,
Sent forth from heaven among the sons of men,
And gone into the boundless heaven again.

The faint old man shall lean his silver head
  To feel thee; thou shalt kiss the child asleep,
And dry the moistened curls that overspread
  His temples, while his breathing grows more deep;
And they who stand about the sick man's bed
  Shall joy to listen to thy distant sweep,

And softly part his curtains to allow
Thy visit, grateful to his burning brow.

Go—but the circle of eternal change,
  Which is the life of Nature, shall restore,
With sounds and scents from all thy mighty range,
  Thee to thy birth-place of the deep once more.
Sweet odors in the sea air, sweet and strange,
  Shall tell the home-sick mariner of the shore;
And, listening to thy murmur, he shall deem
He hears the rustling leaf and running stream.

William Cullen Bryant.

THE ECHOING GREEN.

The sun does arise,
And make happy the skies:
The merry bells ring
To make happy the spring:
The skylark and thrush,
The birds of the bush,
Sing louder around
To the bell's cheerful sound,
While our sports shall be seen
On the echoing green.

Old John, with white hair,
Does laugh away care,
Sitting under the oak,
Among the old folk;
They laugh at our play,
And soon they all say,

Such, such were the joys,
When we all, girls and boys,
In our youth-time were seen
On the echoing green.

Till the little ones, weary,
No more can be merry,
The sun does descend,
And our sports have an end.
Round the laps of their mothers,
Many sisters and brothers,
Like birds in their nest,
Are ready for rest,
And sport no more seen,
On the darkening green.

William Blake.

ODE TO EVENING.

If aught of oaten stop, or pastoral song,
May hope, chaste Eve, to soothe thy modest ear,
Like thy own brawling springs,
Thy springs and dying gales—

O Nymph reserved, while now the bright-haired Sun
Sits in yon western tent, whose cloudy skirts,
With brede ethereal wove,
O'erhang his wavy bed.

Now air is hushed, save where the weak-eyed bat
With short shrill shriek flits by on leathern wing,
Or where the beetle winds
His small but sullen horn,

As oft he rises midst the twilight path,
Against the pilgrim borne in heedless hum;
    Now teach me, maid composed,
    To breathe some softened strain,

Whose numbers, stealing through thy darkening vale,
May not unseemly with its stillness suit;
    As, musing slow, I hail
    Thy genial, loved return!

For when thy folding star arising shows
His paly circlet, at his warning lamp
    The fragrant Hours, and elves
    Who slept in buds the day,

And many a nymph who wreathes her brows with sedge,
And sheds the freshening dew; and, lovelier still,
    The pensive pleasures sweet,
    Prepare thy shadowy car.

Then let me rove some wild and heathy scene;
Or find some ruin midst its dreary dells,
    Whose walls more awful nod
    By thy religious gleams.

Or, if chill blustering winds, or driving rain,
Prevent my willing feet, be mine the hut
    That, from the mountain's side,
    Views wilds, and swelling floods,

And hamlets brown, and dim discovered spires;
And hears their simple bell, and marks o'er all
    Thy dewy fingers draw
    The gradual dusky veil.

While Spring shall pour his showers, as oft he wont,
And bathe thy breathing tresses, meekest Eve!
While Summer loves to sport
Beneath thy lingering light;

While sallow Autumn fills thy lap with leaves;
Or Winter, yelling through the troublous air,
Affrights thy shrinking train,
And rudely rends thy robes;

So long, regardful of thy quiet rule,
Shall Fancy, Friendship, Science, smiling Peace,
Thy gentlest influence own,
And love thy favorite name!

William Collins.

DESCRIPTION OF A SUMMER'S EVE.

Down the sultry arc of day
The burning wheels have urged their way;
And Eve along the western skies
Sheds her intermingling dyes.
Down the deep, the miry lane,
Creaking comes the empty wain,
And driver on the shaft-horse sits,
Whistling now and then by fits;
And oft, with his accustom'd call,
Urging on the sluggish Ball.
The barn is still, the master's gone,
And thresher puts his jacket on,
While Dick, upon the ladder tall,
Nails the dead kite to the wall.

Here comes shepherd Jack at last,
He has penned the sheepcote fast,
For 'twas but two nights before,
A lamb was eaten on the moor;
His empty wallet Rover carries,
Nor for Jack, when near home, tarries.
With lolling tongue he runs to try
If the horse-trough be not dry.
The milk is settled in the pans,
And supper messes in the cans;
In the hovel carts are wheeled,
And both the colts are drove afield;
The horses are all bedded up,
And the ewe is with the tup.
The snare for Mister Fox is set,
The leaven laid, the thatching wet,
And Bess has slinked away to talk
With Roger in the holly walk.
Now on the settle all but Bess,
Are set to eat their supper mess;
And little Tom and roguish Kate
Are swinging on the meadow gate.
Now they chat of various things,
Of taxes, ministers, and kings,
Or else tell all the village news,
How madam did the squire refuse;
How parson on his tithes was bent,
And landlord oft distrain'd for rent.
Thus do they talk, till in the sky
The pale-eyed moon is mounted high,
And from the ale-house drunken Ned
Had reeled, then hasten all to bed.

The mistress sees that lazy Kate
The happing coal on kitchen grate
Has laid—while master goes throughout,
Sees shutters fast, the mastiff out,
The candles safe, the hearths all clear,
And naught from thieves or fire to fear;
Then both to bed together creep,
And join the general troop of sleep.

Henry Kirke White.

THE WOOD-CUTTER'S NIGHT SONG.

Welcome, red and roundy sun,
  Dropping lowly in the west;
Now my hard day's work is done,
  I'm as happy as the best.

Joyful are the thoughts of home;
  Now I'm ready for my chair;
So, till morrow-morning's come,
  Bill and mittens, lie ye there!

Though to leave your pretty song,
  Little birds, it gives me pain,
Yet to-morrow is not long,
  Then I'm with you all again.

If I stop, and stand about,
  Well I know how things will be—
Judy will be looking out
  Every now and then for me.

So fare-ye-well! and hold your tongues;
Sing no more until I come;
They're not worthy of your songs
That never care to drop a crumb.

All day long I love the oaks,
But at nights, yon little cot,
When I see the chimney smokes,
Is by far the prettiest spot.

Wife and children all are there,
To revive with pleasant looks,
Table ready set, and chair,
Supper hanging on the hooks.

Soon as ever I get in,
When my fagot down I fling,
Little prattlers they begin
Teasing me to talk and sing.

Welcome, red and roundy sun,
Dropping lowly in the west;
Now my hard day's work is done,
I'm as happy as the best.

Joyful are the thoughts of home;
Now I'm ready for my chair;
So, till morrow-morning's come,
Bill and mittens, lie ye there!

John Clare.

TO THE NIGHTINGALE.

O Nightingale, that on yon bloomy spray
  Warblest at eve, when all the woods are still,
  Thou with fresh hope the lover's heart dost fill,
While the jolly hours lead on propitious May.
Thy liquid notes, that close the eye of day,
  First heard before the shallow cuckoo's bill,
  Portend success in love. O if Jove's will
Have linked that amorous power to thy soft lay,
Now timely sing, ere the rude bird of hate
  Foretell my hopeless doom in some grove nigh;
  As thou from year to year hast sung too late
For my relief, yet hadst no reason why.
  Whether the Muse or Love call thee his mate,
Both them I serve, and of their train am I.

John Milton.

TO THE EVENING STAR.

Star that bringest home the bee,
And sett'st the weary laborer free!
If any star shed peace, 'tis thou,
  That send'st it from above,
Appearing when Heaven's breath and brow
  Are sweet as hers we love.

Come to the luxuriant skies,
Whilst the landscape's odors rise,
Whilst, far off, lowing herds are heard,
  And songs when toil is done,
From cottages whose smoke unstirred
  Curls yellow in the sun.

Star of love's soft interviews,
Parted lovers on thee muse;
Their remembrancer in Heaven
  Of thrilling vows thou art,
Too delicious to be riven,
  By absence, from the heart.

Thomas Campbell.

Move eastward, happy Earth, and leave
  Your orange sunset waning slow;
From fringes of the faded eve,
  O, happy planet, eastward go;
Till over thy dark shoulder glow
  Thy silver sister-world, and rise
  To glass herself in dewy eyes
That watch me from the glen below.

Ah, bear me with thee, lightly borne,
  Dip forward under starry light,
And move me to my marriage-morn,
  And round again to happy night.

Alfred Tennyson.

SONG.

O welcome, bat, and owlet gray,
Thus winging lone your airy way;
And welcome, moth, and drowsy fly,
That to mine ear come humming by;

And welcome, shadows long and deep,
And stars that from the pale sky peep!
O welcome all! to me ye say,
My woodland love is on her way.
Upon the soft wind floats her hair,
Her breath is in the dewy air;
Her steps are in the whispered sound
That steals along the stilly ground.
O dawn of day, in rosy bower,
What art thou in this witching hour!
O noon of day, in sunshine bright,
What art thou in the fall of night!

Joanna Bailie.

TO THE GLOW-WORM.

Tasteful Illumination of the night,
  Bright scattered, twinkling star of spangled earth!
Hail to thy nameless coloured dark-and-light,
  The witching nurse of thy illumined birth.
In thy still hour how dearly I delight
  To rest my weary bones, from labor free;
In lone spots, out of hearing, out of sight,
  To sigh day's smothered pains; and pause on thee,
  Bedecking dangling brier and ivied tree,
Or diamonds tipping on the grassy spear;
  Thy pale-faced glimmering light I love to see,
Gilding and glistering in the dew-drop near:
  O still-hour's mate! my easing heart sobs free,
While tiny bents low bend with many an added tear.

John Clare.

SONG.—THE OWL.

WHEN cats run home and light is come,
And dew is cold upon the ground,
And the far-off stream is dumb,
And the whirring sail goes round,
And the whirring sail goes round;
Alone and warming his five wits,
The white owl in the belfry sits.

When merry milkmaids click the latch,
And rarely smells the new-mown hay,
And the cock has sung beneath the thatch
Twice or thrice his roundelay,
Twice or thrice his roundelay;
Alone and warming his five wits,
The white owl in the belfry sits.

Alfred Tennyson.

TO CYNTHIA.

QUEEN and huntress, chaste and fair,
Now the sun is laid to sleep,
Seated in thy silver chair,
State in wonted manner keep:
Hesperus entreats thy light,
Goddess excellently bright!

Earth, let not thy envious shade
Dare itself to interpose;
Cynthia's shining orb was made
Heaven to clear when day did close;

Bless us, then, with wishèd sight,
Goddess excellently bright!
Lay thy bow of pearl apart,
  And thy crystal-shining quiver;
Give unto thy flying hart
  Space to breathe, how short soever;
Thou that makest a day of night,
Goddess excellently bright!

Ben Jonson.

ODE TO A NIGHTINGALE.

My heart aches, and a drowsy numbness pains
  My sense, as though of hemlock I had drunk;
Or emptied some dull opiate to the drains
  One minute past, and Lethe-ward had sunk.
'Tis not through envy of thy happy lot,
  But being too happy in thy happiness,
That thou, light-wingèd Dryad of the trees,
    In some melodious plot
  Of beechen green, and shadows numberless,
Singest of Summer in full-throated ease.

Oh for a draught of vintage
  Cooled a long age in the deep-delvèd earth,
Tasting of Flora and the country green,
  Dance, and Provençal song, and sun-burned mirth!
Oh for a beaker full of the warm South,
  Full of the true, the blushful Hippocrene,
With beaded bubbles winking at the brim,
    And purple-stainèd mouth—
  That I might drink, and leave the world unseen,
And with thee fade away into the forest dim.

Fade far away, dissolve, and quite forget
  What thou among the leaves hast never known—
The weariness, the fever, and the fret;
  Here, where men sit and hear each other groan—
Where palsy shakes a few sad, last gray hairs—
  Where youth grows pale, and spectre-thin, and dies—
When but to think is to be full of sorrow
    And leaden-eyed despairs;
  Where Beauty cannot keep her lustrous eyes,
Or new Love pine at them beyond to-morrow.

Away! away! for I will fly to thee,
  Not charioted by Bacchus and his pards,
But on the viewless wings of Poesy,
  Though the dull brain perplexes and retards:
Already with thee! tender is the night,
  And haply the Queen-Moon is on her throne,
Clustered around by all her starry Fays;
    But here there is no light,
  Save what from heaven is with the breezes blown
Through verdurous glooms and winding mossy ways.

I cannot see what flowers are at my feet,
  Nor what soft incense hangs upon the boughs,
But, in embalmèd darkness, guess each sweet
  Wherewith the seasonable month endows
The grass, the thicket, and the fruit-tree wild:
  White hawthorn, and the pastoral eglantine;
Fast-fading violets, covered up in leaves;
    And mid-May's oldest child,
  The coming musk-rose, full of dewy wine,
The murmurous haunt of bees on summer eves.

Darkling I listen; and for many a time
  I have been half in love with easeful Death,
Called him soft names in many a mused rhyme,
  To take into the air my quiet breath;
Now, more than ever, seems it rich to die,
  To cease upon the midnight, with no pain,
While thou art pouring forth thy soul abroad,
    In such an ecstasy!
  Still wouldst thou sing, and I have ears in vain—
To thy high requiem become a sod.

Thou wast not born for death, immortal bird!
  No hungry generations tread thee down;
The voice I hear this passing night was heard
  In ancient days by emperor and clown:
Perhaps the self-same song that found a path
  Through the sad heart of Ruth, when, sick for home.
She stood in tears amid the alien corn:
    The same that oft-times hath
  Charmed magic casements opening on the foam
Of perilous seas, in fairy lands forlorn.

Forlorn! the very word is like a bell,
  To toll me back from thee to my sole self!
Adieu! the Fancy cannot cheat so well
  As she is famed to do, deceiving elf!
Adieu! adieu! thy plaintive anthem fades
  Past the near meadows, over the still stream,
Up the hill-side; and now 'tis buried deep
    In the next valley-glades:
  Was it a vision or a waking dream?
Fled is that music—do I wake or sleep?

John Keats.

NEW BOOKS,

JUST PUBLISHED BY

BUNCE & HUNTINGTON,

No. 540, BROADWAY, NEW YORK.

I.

WHAT TO DO WITH THE COLD MUTTON. A Book of Réchauffé's, with numerous approved Receipts for the kitchen of a Gentleman of moderate income. 1 vol., cloth. Price 80 cts.

II.

PARSON AND PEOPLE; or, Incidents in the Every-Day Life of a Clergyman. By the Rev. EDWARD SPOONER, M. A., Vicar of Heston, Middlesex. With a Preface by an American Clergyman. A book of rare beauty, pathos, and humor, and of uncommon interest for both Clergymen and Laymen. 1 vol., cloth, 16mo, with an illustration. Price $1 25.

III.

OUR FARM OF TWO ACRES. By HARRIET MARTINEAU. Although resembling in title a book published a few years ago, this little book is entirely new. The experiences it records are highly entertaining and suggestive. Paper cover, 48 pp. Price 20 cts.

IV.

GOLDEN LEAVES FROM THE AMERICAN POETS. Collected by JOHN W. S. HOWS. Green vellum cloth, bevelled boards, gilt top, 16mo, 560 pages. Price $2 50.

V.

GOLDEN LEAVES FROM THE BRITISH POETS. Uniform in style and price with "Golden Leaves from the American Poets." Collected by JOHN W. S. HOWS.

These two volumes combined afford, it is believed, the most complete and desirable selection of British and American poetry that has yet been made. The convenient size of the volumes, the beauty of the page, the extreme elegance of their external appearance, unite in commending them to persons of taste.

A third volume, entitled "Golden Leaves from the Dramatic Poets," is in preparation.

VI.

THE MECHANICS', MACHINISTS', AND ENGINEERS' PRACTICAL BOOK OF REFERENCE. By CHARLES HASLETT, Civil Engineer, Edited by Prof. CHARLES W. HACKLEY, late Professor of Mathematics in Columbia College, N. Y. A new edition. 16mo, 520 pp., pocket-book form. Price $2 50.

Any book on this list sent by mail, post free, on receipt of price.

540, BROADWAY, NEW YORK.

BUNCE & HUNTINGTON
HAVE JUST READY:

THE

LINCOLN MEMORIAL:

A RECORD OF THE

LIFE, ASSASSINATION, AND OBSEQUIES

OF THE

MARTYRED PRESIDENT;

Containing a Sketch of the Life of President Lincoln, an accurate account of the Assassination, the particulars of the Obsequies from Washington to Springfield, a report of the Funeral Discourses in the various cities; together with a full account of the assassin's capture and death. It presents in one volume every thing pertaining to the great event worthy of preservation. With a portrait of Mr. Lincoln, and a view of his early home in Kentucky. One volume 8vo, bevelled boards. Price $2.00.

ABRAHAM LINCOLN:

AN HORATIAN ODE.

BY RICHARD HENRY STODDARD.

"A magnificent picture of the nation's tribute of mourning for its dead chief."—*New York Evening Post.*

8vo, paper. Price 25 cents.

SOLDIERS' LETTERS:

A Collection of Letters

FROM SOLDIERS, BOTH OFFICERS AND PRIVATES,

Relating their

PERSONAL ADVENTURES IN THE GREAT REBELLION.

EDITED BY LYDIA MINTURN POST.

The letters contained in this volume were collected by a Committee of Ladies for the Sanitary Commission, in response to an appeal addressed by them to the families of soldiers

They relate those thrilling incidents of heroic adventure and self-sacrificing patriotism, and those peculiar experiences of the MARCH, the BATTLE, and the CAMP, not to be found in the general public accounts, thereby affording a most vivid *inside* view of the War—the hardships, adventures, triumphs, and sufferings of our noble band of Northern heroes, told in their own simple, unaffected, but graphic language.

One vol. 12mo, 468 pp., cloth, gilt back and side. Price $2 00.

BUNCE & HUNTINGTON, PUBLISHERS,
No. 540, Broadway, New York.

www.ingramcontent.com/pod-product-compliance
Lightning Source LLC
LaVergne TN
LVHW021430110826
845150LV00007B/2162

* 9 7 8 1 4 2 5 5 0 7 5 6 5 *